First published in the USA in 2025
by Welbeck Children's Books
An imprint of Hachette Children's Group

Copyright © 2025 Hodder & Stoughton Limited

All rights reserved. This book is sold subject to the condition that it may not be reproduced, stored in a retrieval system, or transmitted in any form or by any means, electronic, mechanical, photocopying, recording, or otherwise, without the publisher's prior consent.

ISBN 978 1 80453 775 6

Printed in China
10 9 8 7 6 5 4 3 2 1

This is not an official Minecraft product.
This book has not been authorised, licensed or endorsed by Microsoft or Mojang Studios, nor by anyone involved in the creation, production or distribution of the Minecraft series of videogames.

All information correct as of November 2024.

Welbeck Children's Books
An imprint of Hachette Children's Group
Part of Hodder & Stoughton Limited
Carmelite House, 50 Victoria Embankment
London EC4Y 0DZ

An Hachette UK Company
www.hachette.co.uk
www.hachettechildrens.co.uk

Builds by Ben Westwood
Special thanks to: Paleschi, Kakashi87, StreetWolfJack

CHALLENGES
MINECRAFT MASTER BUILDER

WELBECK
CHILDREN'S BOOKS

CONTENTS

**WELCOME TO
MINECRAFT CHALLENGES**   06

MULTIPLAYER MINIGAMES   08

RAVE ABOUT REDSTONE   10

CLASSIC GAMES
MINI GOLF   12
CONNECT CONCRETE POWDER 4   14
BATTLE BLAST   18
STEVE SAYS   22
GUESS THAT TUNE   24

PRECISION GAMES
BULLSEYE BATTLE   28
LEAP OF FAITH   29
ARMOR ARCHERY   30
CHICKEN DROP   34
TNT FLOOR   38
DANGER BRIDGE   42
GOLDRUSH   46

RACING GAMES
LAVA RACE	50
CAMEL DASH	51
KING OF THE HILL	52
MICRO PARKOUR MAZE	56

COMBAT GAMES
MINECART JOUSTING	60
ICEBOAT COMBAT ARENA	64
SUMOCRAFT	68
FIRE STARTER	72
SURVIVE THE NIGHT	76

INVENTORY CHECKLIST — 80

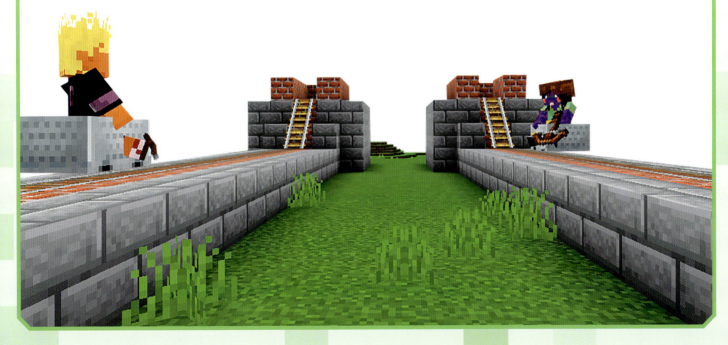

WELCOME TO MINECRAFT CHALLENGES

If you're looking to compete against your Minecraft buddies with exciting builds, then Challenges may be just what you're looking for. You can play minigames in either Survival or Creative mode across a range of settings, and YOU create the games! Let's find out some more . . .

WHAT ARE MINIGAMES?

In a nutshell, **minigames** are small arcade-style games, and this genre has been one of the all-time favorites since Minecraft first launched. As the name suggests, minigames don't go on forever—they last for up to 30 minutes. Ultimately, they are all about building, exploring, and adventure—what's not to love?

TYPES OF MINIGAMES IN THIS BOOK

- **Classic Games:** These games are based on traditional games like "Battleship" but with a Minecraft twist.

- **Precision Games:** These games take a bit more concentration and some fancy footwork. There are archery games that call for precise shooting and parkour games where you need to watch your step.

- **Racing Games:** On your marks! These games will challenge you and your friends to see who comes out on top.

- **Combat Games:** Get ready to fight! In these games you can fight with each other or team up to battle against hostile mobs—take your pick!

CREATE YOUR OWN . . .

The games already out there are cool and stuff, but the real fun begins when you create your own. Did you know that **minigames** can be played solo, splitscreen (on the same console), or online with your friends? All you need to do is harness your creativity and spark your imagination. Having the power to decide how your game works is awesome, and it's such a thrill seeing them played out for real as your friends compete, battle, and (try to) master your world!

HIDE AND SEEK

Why not try playing a game of hide and seek with your Minecraft buddies? Remember it's an infinite world, so you can play it however you want! Just be sure to set some perimeters or things could get more than a little tricky. For example, you could build a village to play it in, or a building, or even an island. It's up to you!

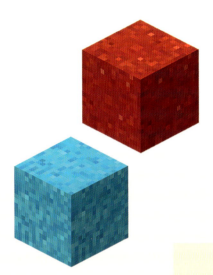

CREATIVE VS. SURVIVAL

- All Minecraft fans are familiar with **Survival mode**—it's the go-to way to play after all and it's tons of fun, too! In **Survival** you need to mine resources and find food while monitoring your health and hunger bars, not to mention dealing with the threat of pesky mobs. That's not to say you can't build **minigames** in **Survival** because you sure can, but it's not without its challenges!

- When it comes to **Creative mode**, things look quite different. For starters, you will have a creative inventory with all the blocks you will possibly need so that you can focus on creating—you don't need to mine for coal or any other resources! What's more, you will also have all the weapons, tools, and armor ready and waiting for you. Pretty cool, huh? Plus, mobs will spawn, but they won't be hostile or attack you in this mode. Handy!

INVENTORY CHECKLIST

Before you get started, flip to page 80 and check out the **inventory checklist** so you can get all your equipment ready for your builds.

MULTIPLAYER MINIGAMES

Minigames are more fun with friends, so be sure to send them an invite when your game is ready to play. Just open the menu and find their account.

PLAYERS

It's a good idea to think about how many players your game will need before you get too far through the planning. Do you want to build a team game? Be sure there is plenty of space and take some time to think about what you will need for each player. Another option would be player v player (PvP), so it's a case of deciding what will suit YOUR game best? Don't be afraid to experiment.

STAYING SAFE

Although Minecraft is all about having fun, the most important thing of all is staying safe. Here are some tips to help you:

- Always ask permission before going online. Tell a trusted adult what you are doing and ask before downloading anything
- Turn off chat
- Find a child-friendly server
- Only screenshare with real-life friends
- Watch out for viruses and malware
- Set a game-play time limit
- Never use your real name
- Never share personal information such as where you live or the school you go to
- Always tell a trusted adult if you see or hear anything worrying

HOW TO PLAY ONLINE

If you want to share your creations with your nearest and dearest, you have a few options. You can start your own server and invite friends to join you, or can join an existing server. Or if you want something a bit more secure then **Realms** is the answer. It's basically a private server for you and any friends and family you want to invite along for the ride!

REALMS

Are you wondering what a **Realm** is? Well, it's basically a subscription to an official Minecraft server just for your family and friends. Here are some important things to know before getting started:

- There are two different versions of **Realms** depending on whether you are using Java or Bedrock edition.
- You need a subscription to create a **Realm** of your own, which means you need an adult's permission.
- You can join a friend's **Realm** without a subscription as only they will need a subscription for you to play. Up to 10 friends can play on a **Realm** together at one time.
- If you make your own **Realm**, this will be the meeting place for your friends and family. So mull over the mode and difficulty settings you think would be best for them and you!

RAVE ABOUT REDSTONE

This humble element is a total game-changer if you want to become a master Minecraft builder! It can be used to build anything from circuits to moving parts . . . this block has it all.

WHAT IS REDSTONE?

It's a block, but with serious potential. You can use **redstone** in **Creative mode** to take your builds to the next level by adding command blocks (see pages 38 and 72). In **Survival mode**, you can still use **redstone**, but it's just more limited. It's a good idea to play around with **redstone** in **Creative** first so you can figure out just what it's capable of!

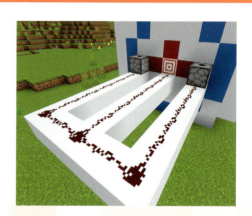

CREATIVE VS SURVIVAL

As with most resources, **redstone** will be given to you if you are playing in **Creative**. But if you're in **Survival**, you will need to mine it from blocks of **redstone ore**. Where do you find that? It's most likely lurking below the surface, so nab yourself an **iron pickaxe** to get the job done.

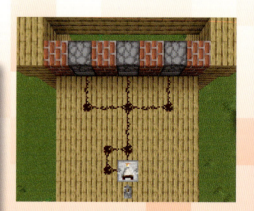

MOVING MECHANISMS

Have you ever wondered how to add moving parts to your Minecraft builds? **Redstone** is the answer.

OTHER WAYS TO USE REDSTONE...

- **Pistons** can push objects around once it has a **redstone signal**
- **Doors** can be made automatic by using **redstone**
- **Pressure plates** let off a **redstone signal** when they are stepped on

TOP TIP

Some of the builds in this book require you to hide your **redstone** circuits. Remember—when covering your redstone, make sure that you never disturb the line of dust. Cutting off the flow will stop your contraptions from working.

REDSTONE TOOLS

REDSTONE TORCH
a power source that can be turned on or off

REDSTONE DUST
acts as a power cable between components

REDSTONE REPEATER
helps maintain **redstone** power

REDSTONE COMPARATOR
used in circuits to lower or maintain signal strength

REDSTONE LEVER
how you turn the power on and off

BLOCK OF REDSTONE
equivalent to nine lines of **redstone dust**

CLASSIC GAMES

MINI GOLF

PLAYER COUNT: 1-10

Follow these steps to create one basic mini golf hole, but don't let that hold you back—you could build a whole 18-hole course. It's time to tee off!

STEP 1

Layout a curved path of **packed ice** with a **brick** boundary like the image below. The **packed ice** path needs to be three blocks wide, but can be as long as you want—you could create several holes of increasing complexity.

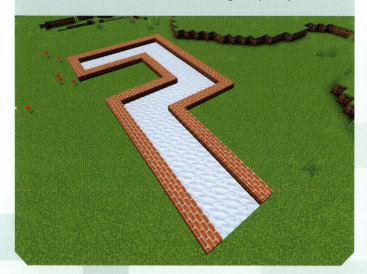

STEP 2

Cover the **packed ice** with **green carpet** to make it look like fake grass. Even though the ice is covered with carpet, if you drop a **snowball** on the course, it will slide around just like it would on ice.

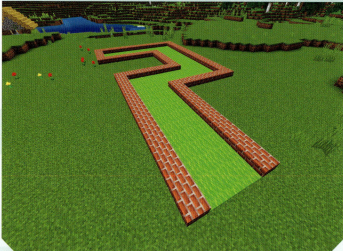

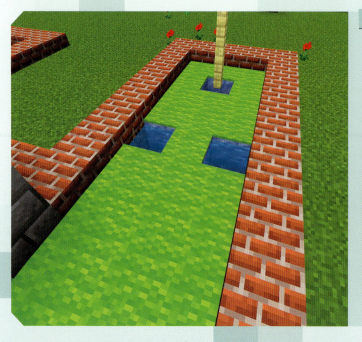

STEP 3

Make a hole at the end of the course and place a **dispenser** in it with a **pressure plate** on top. This will set off a **firework** on a successul putt. Create a couple of water hazards.

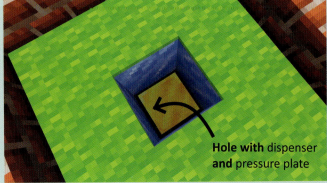

Hole with dispenser **and** pressure plate

DID YOU KNOW?

Golf is full of weird terms. If you get the ball in the hole in the expected number of strokes, it counts as a "par." One stroke over is a "bogey" and one under is a "birdie." Pretty fly, huh?

STEP 4

Add sandy bunkers and build arches out of **stone brick blocks** for players to dodge and navigate, just like on a mini golf course IRL.

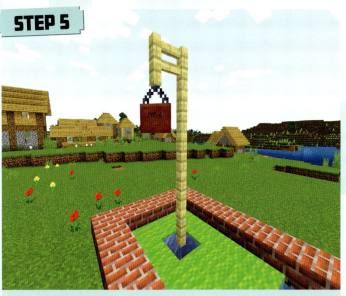

STEP 5

Place an end flag above the hole using **fencing**. You can add a **sign** to it to let competitors know how many shots it should take to get to the end.

CLASSIC GAMES

CONNECT CONCRETE POWDER 4

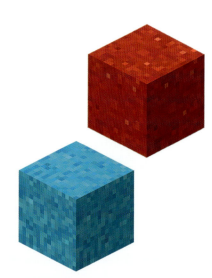

What happens when Connect 4 meets Minecraft? This game lets you drop blocks to try and get four in a row before your opponent. Here's how to get started . . .

STEP 1

For the first stage of your build, lay down some **glass blocks**. We've made ours seven blocks long, but you can make yours bigger. It's up to you!

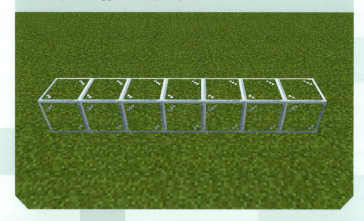

STEP 2

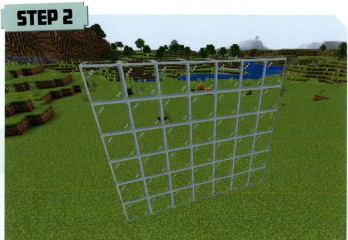

Then build up a whole wall of **glass blocks**, like this. Ours is six blocks high, but go higher if you want to.

STEP 3

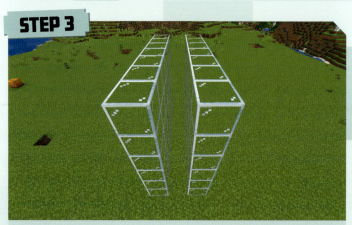

Leaving a one block gap, build another wall of **glass blocks** that is exactly the same size as the first. Your pieces will drop down the gap in the middle, and you will be able to see them through the glass.

STEP 4

Use any color of **concrete blocks** to close up the gaps at each end and create a frame, like this.

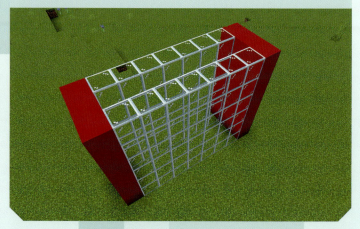

STEP 5

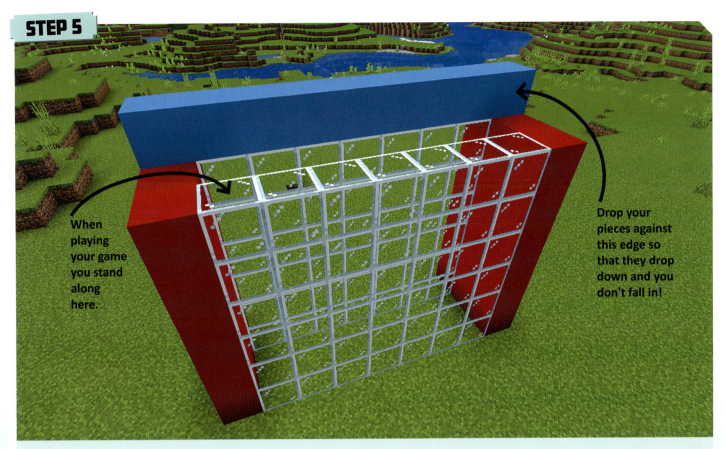

When playing your game you stand along here.

Drop your pieces against this edge so that they drop down and you don't fall in!

Then add another layer of **concrete blocks** right along the top edge of one wall of **glass blocks**.

STEP 6

Next build a platform in a different color that comes out from the opposite side.

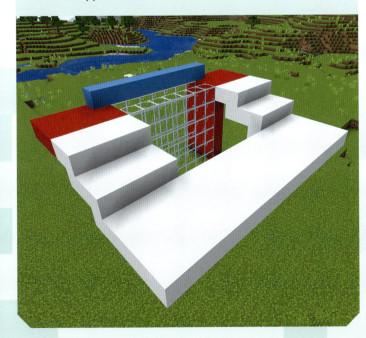

STEP 7

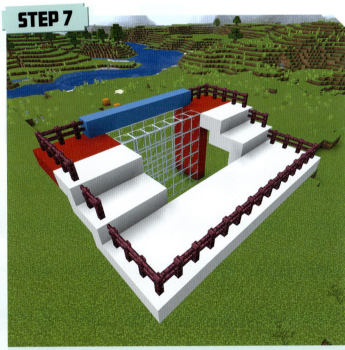

Use a row of **fencing** all the way around the edges. Safety first!

CLASSIC GAMES

STEP 8

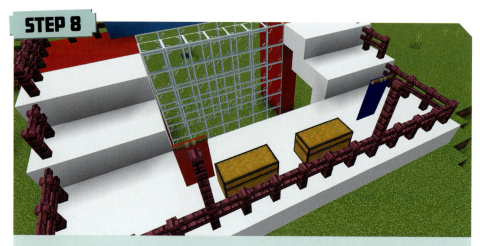

Add two **banners** in different colors to show which player is on which side. We are using blue and red pieces, so we have chosen one red **banner** and one blue **banner**. Then place two **large chests** near the **banners**.

STEP 9

Fill each **large chest** with your players' peices. One **chest** is filled with **red concrete powder** and the other is filled with **blue concrete powder**.

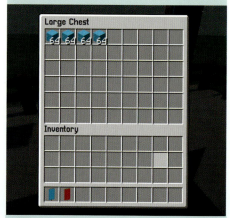

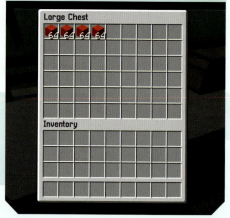

STEP 10

Make a space down the middle of the glass walls so that you can enter. That's where we will build the section that will allow you to reset your game for another round.

STEP 11

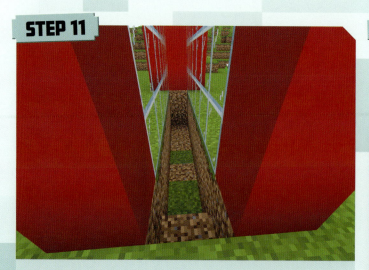

Start by digging down in the middle of the frame. This is two blocks deep.

STEP 12

When you have finished digging out the middle, you can start laying **torches** across the bottom. These **torches** will "mine" your **concrete powder** when it lands on them, essentially making them disappear.

STEP 13

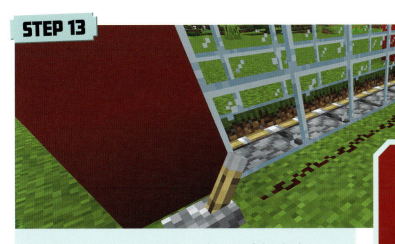

Lay **pistons** at ground level along the top of the ditch you just built. Behind this, you need to add a line of **redstone dust**. Add a **lever** that will turn on the **redstone** power to your **pistons** pushing them out.

STEP 14

When your game is over, you can flip the **lever** back and the **pistons** will retract making the pieces you have played with drop down. This will clear your game so that you are ready to play again.

Add a ladder up the other side so that your players can get to the top.

CLASSIC GAMES

BATTLE BLAST

If you love Battleship, then just you wait till you try Battle Blast! In this exciting game, you must use coordinates to destroy all bombs on your enemy's grid. And this is how to get things started . . .

STEP 1

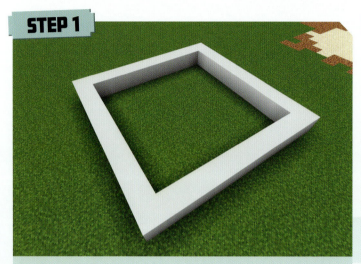

First build a 10 by 10 square using **white concrete blocks**. This will become the main grid that you play on.

STEP 2

Then replace every other block with a contrasting color, like this. Now your grid is taking shape.

STEP 3

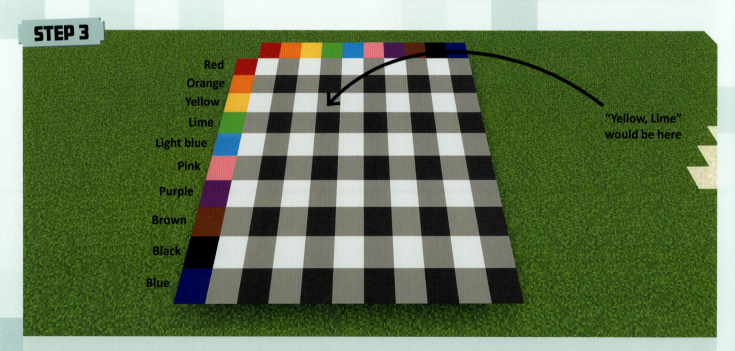

"Yellow, Lime" would be here

In regular Battleship there are numbers going down each side, but in Minecraft we will use a **concrete** color grid. So instead of shouting coordinates, such as "4, 5," you will shout colors. For example, "Yellow, Lime." Make sense?

MINECRAFT MASTER BUILDER: CHALLENGES

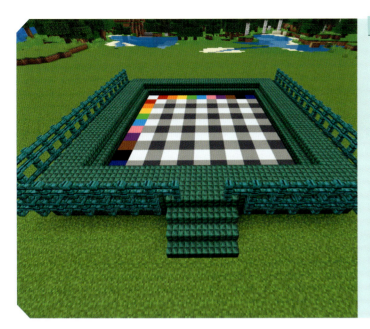

STEP 4

Build up your platform to create more of a stage, as shown. We used **prismarine blocks**, **fencing**, and **stairs** to make it extra fancy! Just be sure to remove any fencing from the far end as this is where your dividing wall will be.

Dividing wall will go here

STEP 5

Build a dividing wall so that the other player will not be able to see where you have placed your pieces. Make this wall six blocks high.

STEP 6

Stand back and have a look at your build so far. This is how your first section should now look.

STEP 7

Now you need to repeat the first steps to build another grid on the other side of the wall. This is how it should look when you have finished.

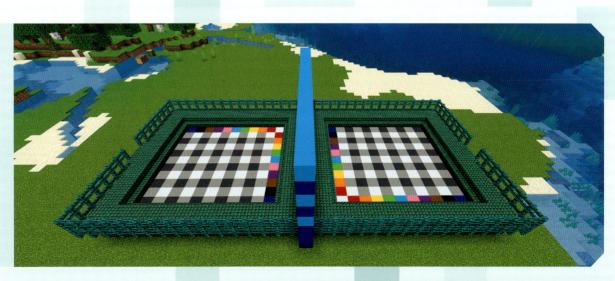

CLASSIC GAMES

STEP 8

Hang a **sign** in the center and a **lectern** where you can place some instructions. There will also need to be a **chest** filled with your pieces. For each game you will need 16 **dispensers**, 16 **fireworks**, and 16 **levers**. We've also included red and green **carpet** so that you can mark the position that each player guesses. Do this by placing a piece of **carpet** over the **dispenser** that has been targeted.

DID YOU KNOW?

In 1979, Battleship was one of the first tabletop games to be reproduced as a video game.

When a **lever** is pulled, your opponent will see the firework **appear above the dividing wall and know they have made a hit!**

STEP 9

It's time to lay your pieces. First fill each **dispenser** with a **firework**. In traditional Battleship, the ships are between two and five spaces long. In this game we are using **dispensers** in place of ships. So lay your 16 **dispensers** out in lines of two to five, like this.

STEP 10

Once you have laid out your **dispensers**, you need to place a **lever** next to each one. When your opponent correctly guesses one of your spots, pull the **lever** to make a **firework** go off. Keep playing until one player discovers all the pieces on their opponent's board.

MINECRAFT MASTER BUILDER: CHALLENGES

STEP 11

When you have followed all of these steps, this is how your build should look. Then it's time to let the real fun begin!

STEP 12

Try adding lights and **lanterns** to play at night. That way your **fireworks** will really shine.

CLASSIC GAMES

PLAYER COUNT: 2-10

STEVE SAYS

One player will be "Steve" and they will be in charge of the dispenser which shoots out colorful fireworks. Players must then race to a bed of that color! Sound fun? Here's how to get started!

STEP 1

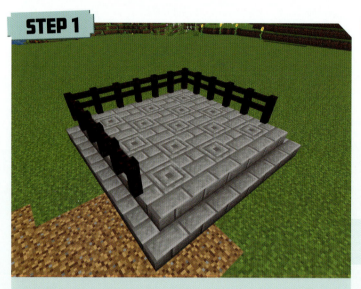

Find a reasonably big open space and build a platform. We used **stone brick blocks** and **chiseled stone** with **stone brick stairs** around the edges and **dark oak fencing**.

STEP 2

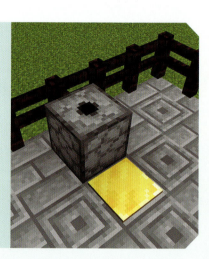

Then place a **dispenser** and a **pressure plate** on the platform. Players must nominate someone to be "Steve" who will be in charge of the **dispenser** and keeping score.

STEP 3

Next fill your **dispenser** with nine different colors of **fireworks**. When stepped on by "Steve," the **pressure plate** will release the **fireworks** in a random order.

STEP 4

Now place a semi circle of nine **beds** in front of your platform. The **beds** must correspond with the colors of the fireworks in your **dispenser**. Then add a starting square in the centre. The green space is where the players gather to begin the game—they should not stand on the red edges!

MINECRAFT MASTER BUILDER: CHALLENGES

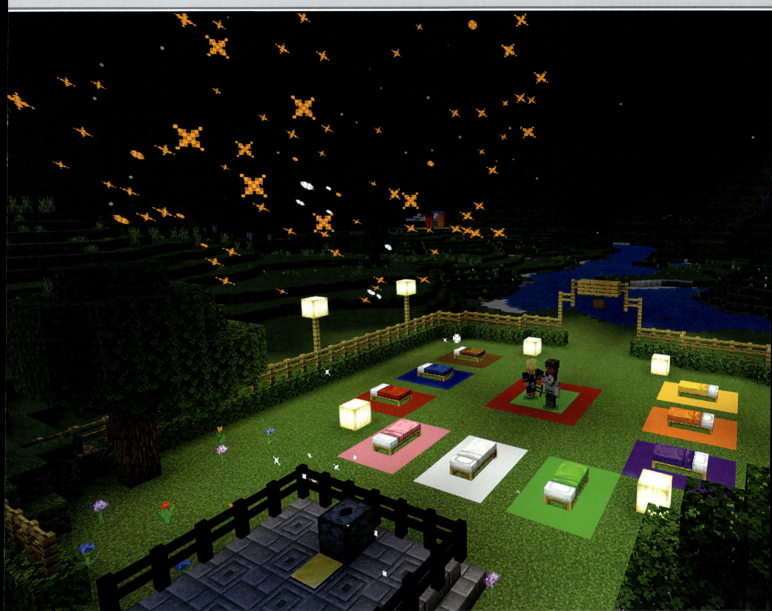

STEP 5

Place a matching color of **concrete** under all your beds so that the colors really stand out. Then decorate the area however you like!

STEP 6

It might be best to play the game at night so that the **fireworks** really stand out! With this in mind, make sure you include lots of light sources.

CLASSIC GAMES

PLAYER COUNT: 2-10

GUESS THAT TUNE

Calling all musical maestros! For this game, one player reads out the numbers while another hits the corresponding piano keys. The aim of the game is to guess the tune being played. Hit it, maestro . . .

STEP 1

Using black and white **concrete blocks**, begin laying out your piano keys. It is important that your keys match the ones shown in Step 4. Each block represents the width and height of one key, and they are three blocks long.

STEP 2

Behind your keys, lay a line of blocks based on how you would like your piano to sound. We used **emerald blocks** for an electronic sound.

This only works if these blocks are placed below a note block.

Here is a list of the different blocks and the sounds they will create when placed under your note blocks.

BLOCK TYPE	SOUND
Emerald	Electronic 8-bit
Wooden	String bass
Glass, Sea lantern	High-hat
Stone, Quartz, Sandstone, Ore, Coral, Brick	Bass drum
Gold	Bell
Clay	Flute
Packed ice	Chime
Wool	Guitar
Bone	Xylophone
Iron	Iron xylophone
Soul sand	Cow bell
Normal (not carved) pumpkin	Didgeridoo
Hay bale	Banjo
Glowstone	Electric piano
Sand, Gravel, Concrete powder	Snare drum
Any block not mentioned	Harp

STEP 3

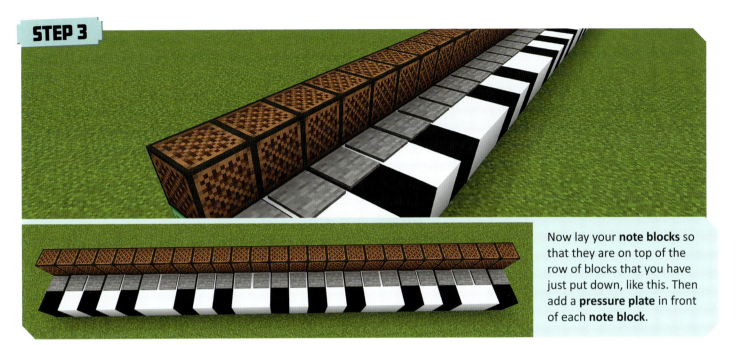

Now lay your **note blocks** so that they are on top of the row of blocks that you have just put down, like this. Then add a **pressure plate** in front of each **note block**.

STEP 4

Make sure that you tune your keys. You can use this as a reference.

How many times to hit "use" or right-click on a note to get a specific note.

0	1	2	3	4	5	6	7	8	9	10	11	12	13	14	15	16	17	18	19	20	21	22	24
F#	G	G#	A	A#	B	C	C#	D	D#	E	F	F#	G	G#	A	A#	B	C	C#	D	D#	E	F#

The music note this block will represent

To tune **note blocks** you need to hit "use" or right click a specific number of times to get a specific note.

STEP 5

Next it's time for you to decorate your keyboard. We have used a combination of **dark oak plank blocks** and **stairs**, but you can choose whatever you want. Make sure you leave a space of one block going back from your **note blocks**.

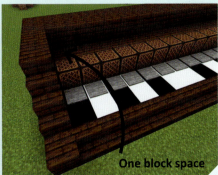

One block space

CLASSIC GAMES

STEP 6

Add a sign to each block behind your **note blocks**. This is where you will add a number to each of your blocks.

STEP 7

One player will be nominated to read out the music notes for the other players. Add a **lectern** for this important player to stand behind. They can read sheet music there if you choose to create it.

STEP 8

Don't forget to add a **ladder** and a **door** for your player to enter.

DID YOU KNOW?

If a **note block** is played repeatedly, it can be used to keep allays close by and encourage them to drop collected items.

MINECRAFT MASTER BUILDER: CHALLENGES

Here are some simple songs to get you started. The music notes have been converted into numbers that will correspond with the notes on your keyboard. Alternatively, you can create your own from existing music . . . depending on how complicated you want to get!

HAPPY BIRTHDAY

1	1	3	1	6	5	
1	1	3	1	8	6	
1	1	2	10	6	5	3
11	11	10	6	8	6	

TWINKLE TWINKLE LITTLE STAR

1	1	8	8	10	10	8
6	6	5	5	3	3	1
8	8	6	6	5	5	3
8	8	6	6	5	5	3
1	1	8	8	10	10	8
6	6	5	5	3	3	1

OLD MACDONALD

6	6	6	1	3	3	1					
10	10	8	8	6							
1	6	6	6	1	3	3	1				
10	10	8	8	6							
1	1	6	6	6	1	1	6	6	6		
6	6	6	6	6	6	6	6	6	6	6	6
6	6	6	1	3	3	1					
10	10	8	8	6							

ROW YOUR BOAT

6	6	6	8	10							
10	8	10	11	1							
7	7	7	1	1	1	10	10	10	6	6	6
1	11	10	8	6							

PRECISION GAMES

BULLSEYE BATTLE

Take aim and hone your archery skills with this target practice game. Challenge a friend to see who can hit the sweet spot most often.

THE LOWDOWN

It shouldn't take long to build an archery range like this, but to make it more "explosive," you need to go around the back . . .

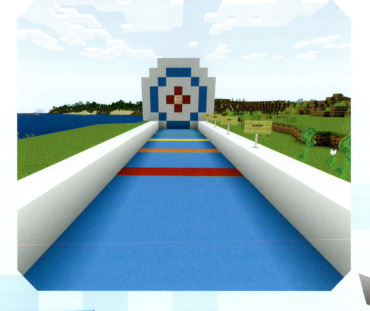

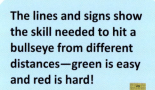

The lines and signs show the skill needed to hit a bullseye from different distances—green is easy and red is hard!

STEP 1

Behind the range, link the back of a **target block** to two **dispensers** as shown below. The redstone dust "wire" is 15 blocks in length from the **target block**, which means only a successful bullseye will give a strong enough signal to power the **dispensers**.

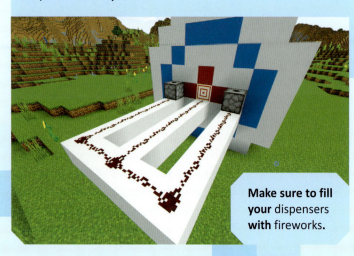

Make sure to fill your dispensers with fireworks.

STEP 2

If your aim is a bit off, nothing will happen. When you hit a bullseye, the **dispensers** will shoot **fireworks** into the air to celebrate your immense skill with a bow!

LEAP OF FAITH

Do you like the idea of jumping off a tall tower, then bouncing down a heap of slime blocks? Let's get started . . .

STEP 1

First of all, you will need to build a super high tower stretching up into the sky. We used lots of different **colored concrete blocks**! The tower is in the shape of a cross and is three blocks by three blocks.

STEP 2

At the top of the tower, build a platform with enough space for six **beds**. This will be where your players start. If they die while falling, they will also return here to respawn in a **bed**.

STEP 3

Now you need to strategically place **slime block** platforms all the way down, like this. When a player jumps, they will have to aim very carefully in order to bounce off a **slime block** and avoid falling.

STEP 4

Place an end goal right at the bottom to give players a target. It's a good idea to do this in water so that they can splash their way to safety.

THE LOWDOWN

If you aren't phased by heights, then you may be just the player to take on this slime-tastic and seriously daring game.

PRECISION GAMES

PLAYER COUNT: 1–10

ARMOR ARCHERY

With this epic game, you can practice your shooting by aiming and firing arrows at moving targets.

STEP 1

Build a base for your archery range. Ours is five blocks wide at the front end, then 13 blocks wide and four blocks deep at the other end. We used **white concrete blocks**.

STEP 2

At the front end, add a **redstone comparator** and be sure it's switched to subtraction mode. Then lay **redstone dust** with a **redstone repeater**—this should be roughly two blocks further down.

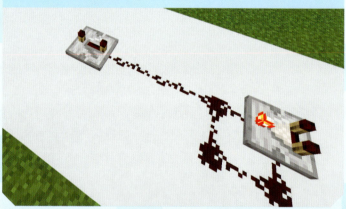

STEP 3

Continuing on from the **repeater**, add another block's worth of **redstone dust**. Use this to create a fork of **redstone dust** with one line in the middle and one at each side. There should be a one block gap between them.

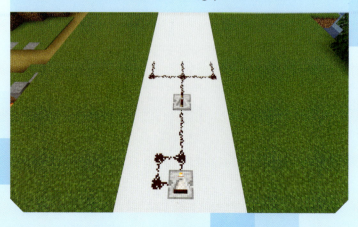

STEP 4

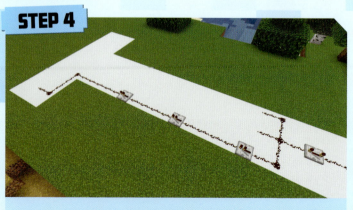

Now add **redstone dust** and **repeaters** along the first line leading around the end of your archery range. Leave a one block gap from the edge and back, like this.

STEP 5

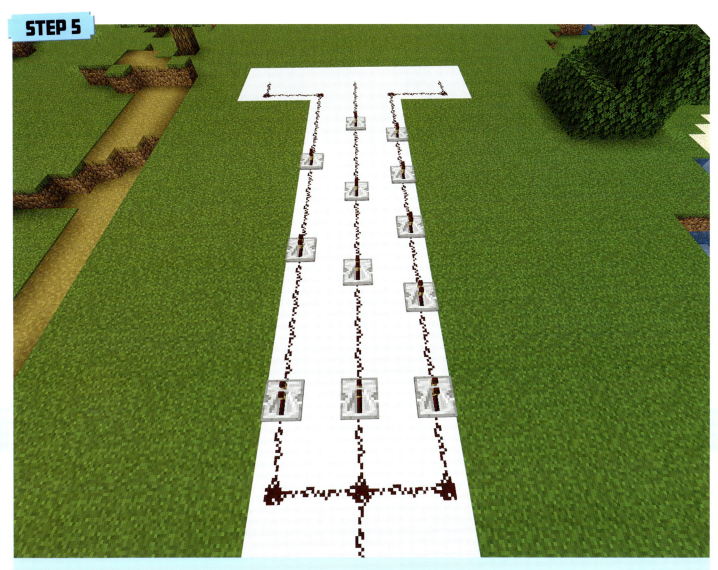

Repeat this process for the other two lines and place the **repeaters** at random intervals. This will mean that your end targets will be moving at different speeds!

STEP 6

At the end of your first line add a **sticky piston**.

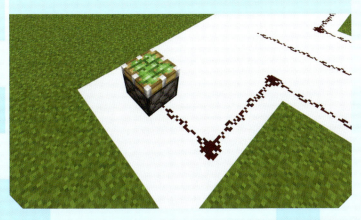

STEP 7

On top of the **sticky piston**, you will need to add an **armor stand**.

PRECISION GAMES

STEP 8

Now do the same for the other two lines so that it looks like this.

STEP 9

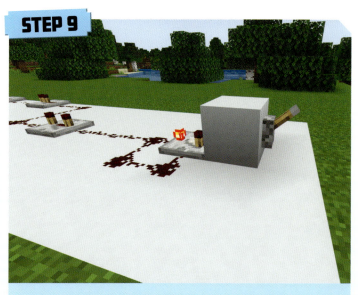

Place a **block** and a **lever** behind your **comparator**.

STEP 10

Flip the **lever** to test out your contraption before you attempt to play. Your **sticky pistons** should shoot your **armor stands** up into the air at different rates.

MINECRAFT MASTER BUILDER: CHALLENGES

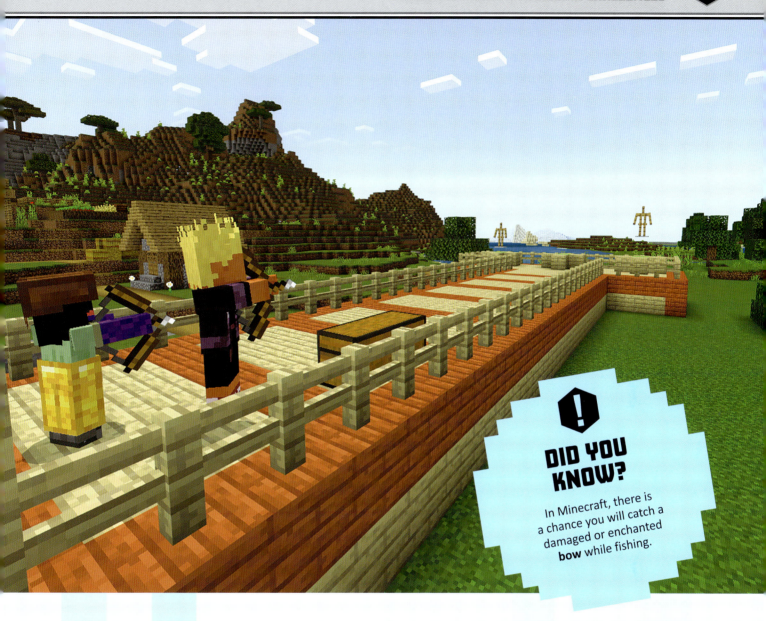

DID YOU KNOW?

In Minecraft, there is a chance you will catch a damaged or enchanted **bow** while fishing.

STEP 11

Start to decorate your build by adding **stairs** at the entrance. We used **acacia plank blocks** and **birch wood stairs**, but you can choose whatever you like. Make sure you leave a gap between your **stairs** so that you have access to the **lever**.

STEP 12

Finish decorating by adding a walkway across the top of your **redstone**, then **fencing** and **banners**. Ready, aim, fire!

PRECISION GAMES

PLAYER COUNT: 2-10

CHICKEN DROP

In this game, players must watch out for dispensers dropping eggs and the goal is to shoot as many chickens as you can . . . Eggs-cellent!

STEP 1

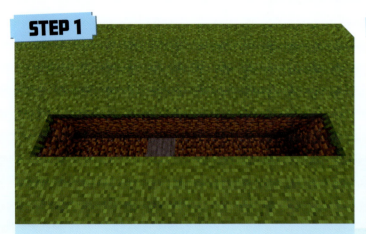

First, dig out a rectangle shape that is seven blocks wide and two blocks deep.

STEP 2

Then fill the hole with **lava**. Now anything that drops down into it cannot escape and will be caught in the **lava**!

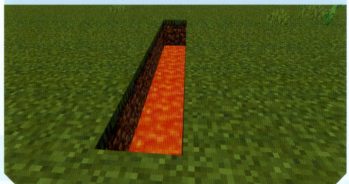

STEP 3

Build up a wall along one side of your **lava**-filled rectangle. Ours is ten blocks high and made from **brick blocks**.

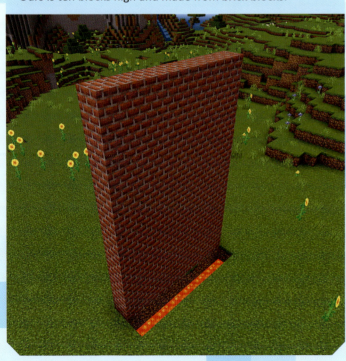

STEP 4

Now you need to build a frame around the wall, as shown in the picture. We made ours two blocks deep and used **oak plank blocks**.

STEP 5

Use **hay bales** to line the bottom front of your frame. Then add a tiered roof right across the top.

STEP 6

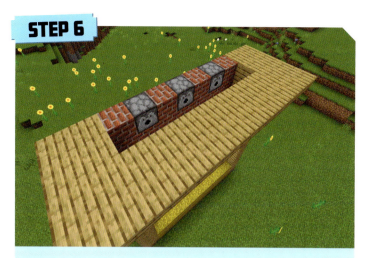

Now add three **dispensers** along the top line of your wall. Be sure to leave a space directly in front of the **dispensers** so that when the **eggs** come out they will drop down and not get blocked!

STEP 7

Then build a platform behind your wall, like this. Add **redstone dust** leading out from your **dispensers** to a **redstone comparator**. Then turn your **comparator** to subtract mode and add a **lever**.

PRECISION GAMES

STEP 8

It's time to fill your **dispensers** with **eggs**!

STEP 9

This is how your game will look once it's been activated. You can either gather your players and start play from here, or you can follow the next steps to ramp it up a bit.

! DID YOU KNOW?

In Minecraft, each **egg** only has a 12.5% chance of spawning a chick!

STEP 10

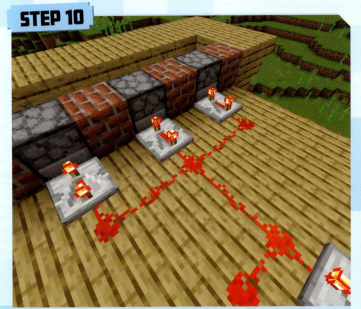

Why not add **redstone repeaters** behind your **dispensers**? This will change the pace that the **eggs** are dropped at and keep players on their toes!

STEP 11

Or you could add more **redstone dust** leading down to the ground along with more **repeaters**. Don't forget to move the **lever** to the front at ground level. This will also change the pace your **eggs** are droppped at and will allow you to start the game without climbing to the top.

STEP 12

Remember that you can cover your **redstone** if you don't want it out in the open. Then enjoy adding some decoration to your game.

STEP 13

You could try adding **fencing** to separate the wall into smaller sections. It's up to you!

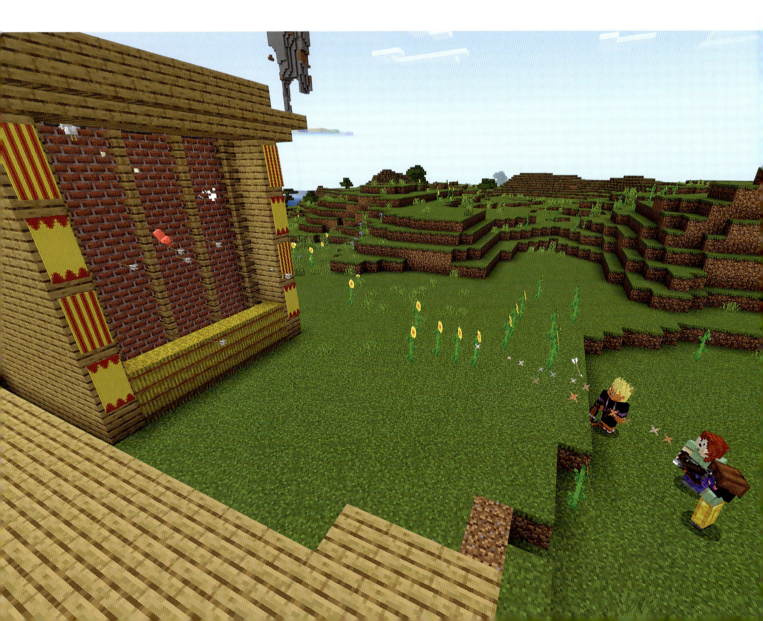

PRECISION GAMES

PLAYER COUNT: 2-10

TNT FLOOR

In this game, a player hides TNT under a platform! The other players must take one step at a time trying to avoid stepping on the TNT.

STEP 1

You will need to find a nice open space that you can build above.

Using command blocks means you can do a simple reset when the game is over without having to rebuild the whole thing to play again.

STEP 2

Put down three **command blocks** floating in mid-air. The bottom block needs a two-block gap above it with two more **command blocks** placed on top on each other.

STEP 3

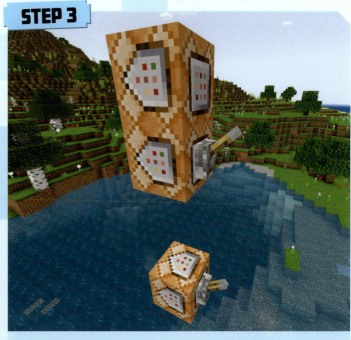

Then add **levers** to the bottom two **command blocks**, like this.

STEP 4

Put the command shown below into the bottom two **command blocks**. This will build your platforms.

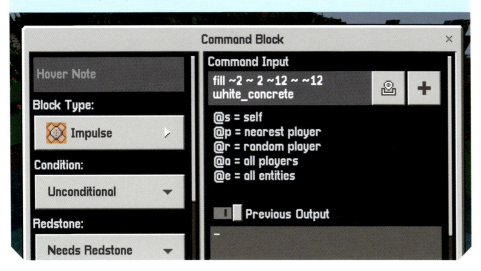

STEP 5

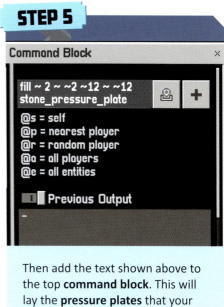

Then add the text shown above to the top **command block**. This will lay the **pressure plates** that your players will be stepping on.

STEP 6

Flip the **levers** on your **command blocks** and your platforms will be built as shown.

PRECISION GAMES

STEP 7

It's wise to surround your build (especially the **command blocks**) with **obsidian blocks**. This will protect them from the **TNT**.

STEP 8

Now you will need to add **ladders** for your players to climb up.

STEP 9

Don't forget to surround your **ladders** with **obsidian**, too.

STEP 10

Build a cool platform for your "games master." They will be the nominmated player who will oversee the game. This player is also the one who places the **TNT**.

STEP 11

The "games master" will climb onto the bottom platform and place a block of **TNT** under the platform above.

STEP 12

Now you are ready to play! Remember that once the placed **TNT** is stepped on, your platform will explode and the game will be over.

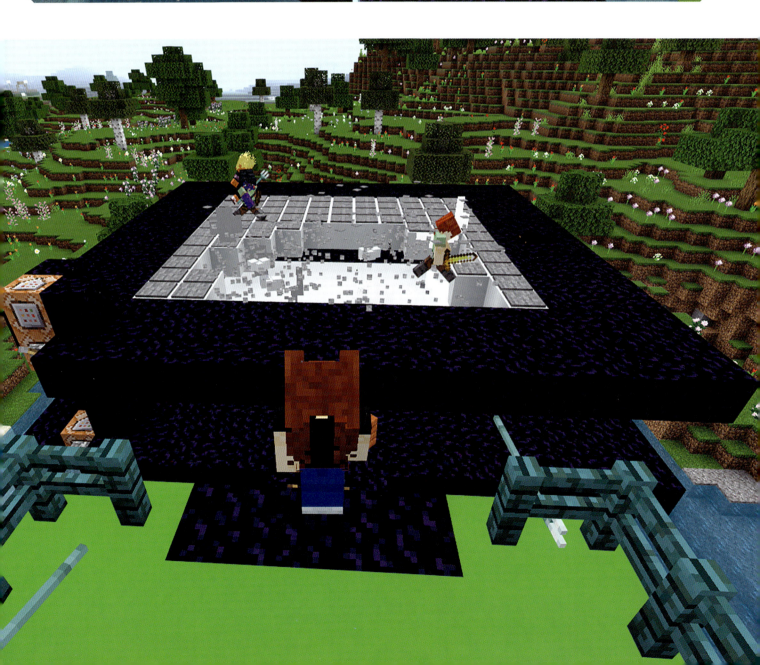

PRECISION GAMES

PLAYER COUNT: 2–10

DANGER BRIDGE

Navigate your way across a bridge over lava by dodging the pistons as you go! A "games master" decides how many blocks will be powered to push off a player. As this is in the nether, there are no beds so once you fall . . . there's no going back!

DID YOU KNOW?
Lava is deadly in Minecraft, but you can swim through it if you drink a fire-resistance potion. Watch out though, the potion effects don't last long!

STEP 1

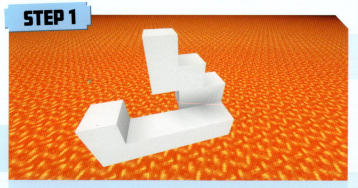

Use **white concrete** to build this structure so that it's hovering up above the lava.

STEP 2

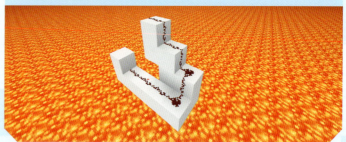

Lay **redstone dust** right along the top of your structure, but leave the first block clear, like this.

STEP 3

Attach a **sticky piston** to the top block so that it's facing toward the first block.

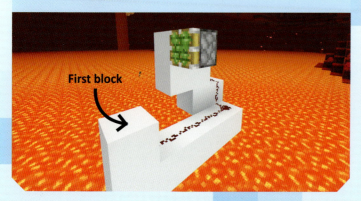

First block

STEP 4

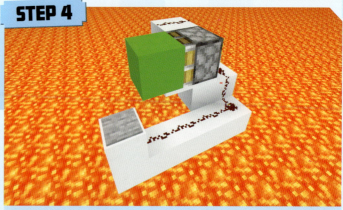

Add a **pressure plate** to the first block. This will activate the **redstone**. Then attach a block to the **sticky piston**—we used a **lime concrete block** for this.

STEP 5

Now build a wall around your **concrete block**—we used **blue concrete blocks** here. You need to leave a gap for the **pressure plate** to poke through.

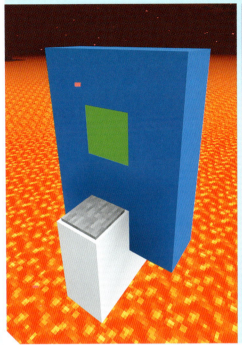
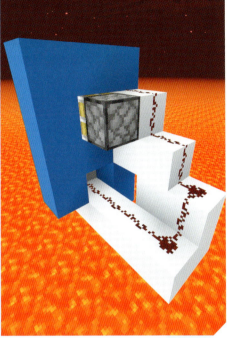

STEP 6

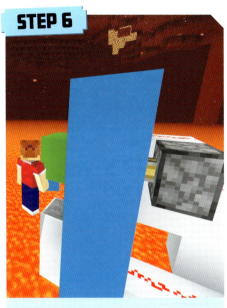

Test out your circuit by stepping on the **pressure plate**. This should make your **sticky piston** push out and force the **green concrete block** to come out beyond your wall. When put to use, this will push a player off of their platform into the lava!

STEP 7

Now you know that your contraption works, you can start designing. We replaced our **blue concrete blocks** with **polished blackstone brick blocks**, and switched the block with the **pressure plate** on with a **chiseled stone block**.

Build a repeat of your contraption opposite this one. Leave a three-block gap between the **pressure plates**. Build the first platform for players to jump on and be sure it has a two-block gap between it and the **pressure plates**. A player will jump between the platforms to the **pressure plates**. When these are activated, they push the player off. The player must guess which **pressure plates** are safe!

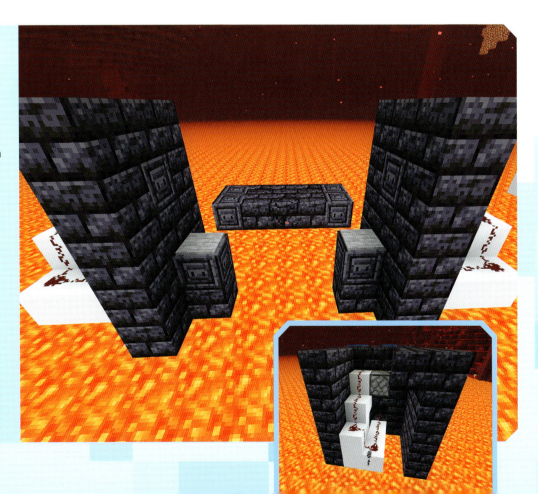

PRECISION GAMES

STEP 8

Build up the walls around your **redstone** to keep it well covered.

STEP 9

Repeat these steps depending on how long you want your bridge to be. Leave a two-block gap between each platform and **pressure plate**. Ours is five **redstone** contraptions long.

STEP 10

Build a walkway along the side of your birdge to enable the "games master" to walk along and adjust the **redstone**.

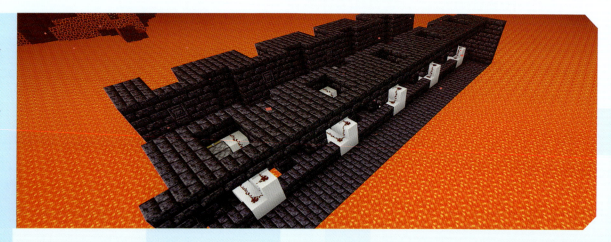

STEP 11

The "games master" will decide which **pressure plates** will be activated and how many. To turn the **pressure plates** on and off all the "games master" needs to do is add and remove a line of **redstone**, as shown below.

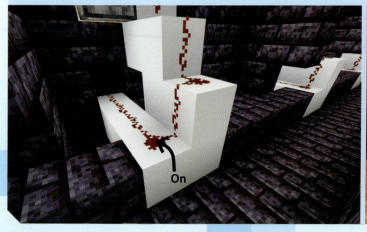

STEP 12

Add a cool **nether portal** to the end of your bridge! This will send the winner back to the overworld.

STEP 13

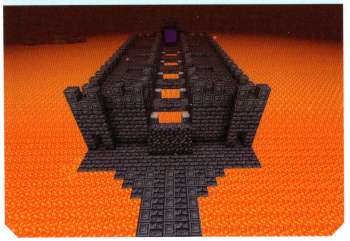

Finally, build a walkway that leads all the way up to your danger bridge.

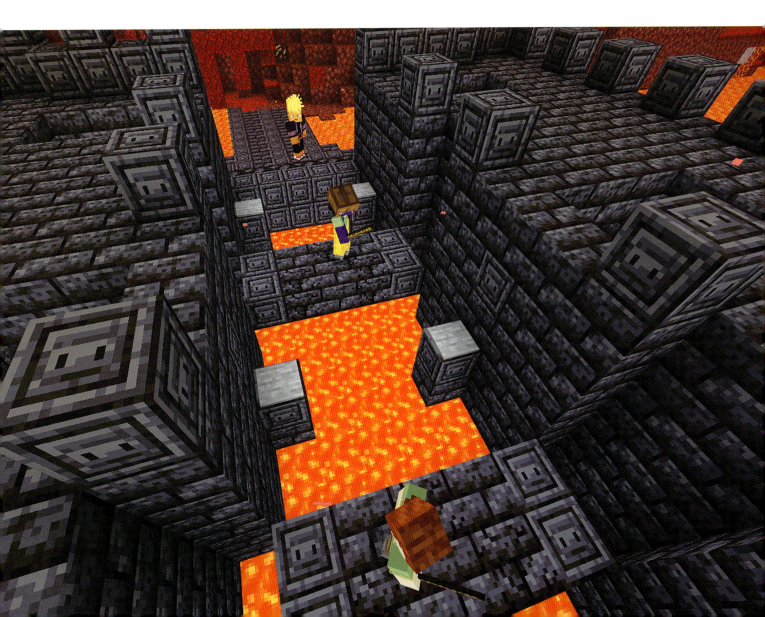

PRECISION GAMES

GOLDRUSH

PLAYER COUNT: 1-10

Wade your way up the course to gather the most golden apples. Are you ready to take the plunge?

STEP 1

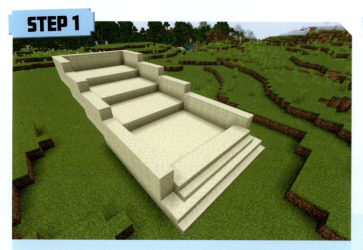

Build a tiered course, like this, for your players to climb. For ours, we used both **sandstone blocks** and **sandstone stairs**.

STEP 2

When your course is all set up, fill it up with **water**.

STEP 3

Add four **droppers** at the top of the course, as shown above.

STEP 4

Then you can fill your **droppers** with items. The goal is to find **golden apples**, so we have filled all but one slot with **red apples**. This makes the golden ones harder to find!

STEP 5

At the bottom of your course, add a **redstone comparator** that is turned to subtraction mode. Now lay a path of **redstone dust** that leads onto two **repeaters**, plus a **lever** to turn it on.

STEP 6

Keep adding **redstone dust** and **repeaters** to each level so that they reach all the way up to the top, as shown here.

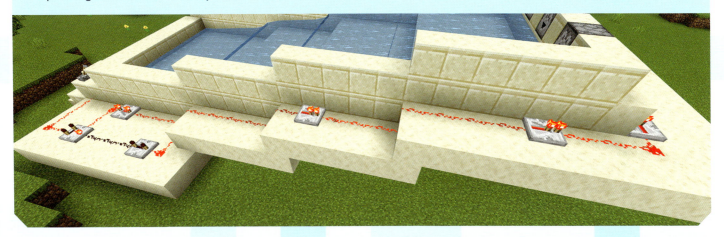

STEP 7

Now add another **repeater** so that you can join up the **redstone dust** to each of your **droppers**. It should now look something like this.

DID YOU KNOW?

A **golden apple** can cure a zombie villager.

PRECISION GAMES

STEP 8

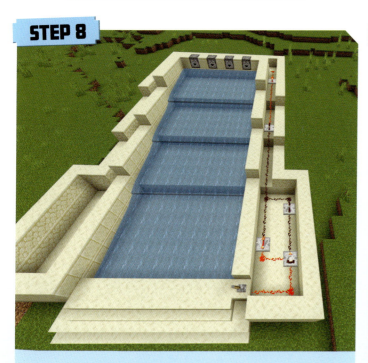

You can keep building up around your **redstone** to hide it while decorating your course. Just make sure the **lever** is accessible at all times.

STEP 9

When covering your **redstone dust**, be careful not to cut anything off! Remember that the **redstone** will not work if you interrupt the flow.

STEP 10

Now it's time to get creative! Have some fun decorating your build and playing around with how it looks. We used **purpur blocks** for additional decoration.

MINECRAFT MASTER BUILDER: CHALLENGES

RACING GAMES

LAVA RACE

Player Count: 2-10

Challenge your friends to speed through the Nether in a high-risk race that's too hot to handle!

STEP 1

You have to ride on Striders for this game. **Striders** can walk on lava without taking damage or sinking, so they make the perfect mount for this race. You just need to saddle them and use a **warped fungus** on a **stick** to steer.

STEP 2

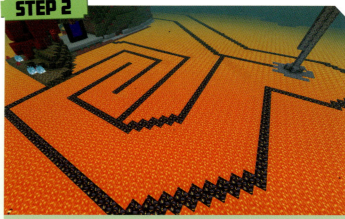

Carefully lay out parallel lines of **cobblestone blocks** to create the track. You can make it as simple or complex as you like—anything from a basic circuit to a twisty path with plenty of hairpin bends.

STEP 3

Try introducing obstacles to navigate. To make the track harder we have included **skeletons**, **blazes**, **magma blocks**, **piglins**, and pillars of **lava**!

THE LOWDOWN

What could be more fun than jumping on a Lava Strider and racing your friends across a stretch of burning-hot lava while exploring the Nether? This is a simple but satisfying racetrack.

CAMEL DASH

The good thing about camels is they can carry two people, no problem! So team up to race your camels through this obstacle-ridden track.

THE LOWDOWN

If you bring the speed (and a bit of daring), it's easy to get over the hump on this game.

STEP 1

First build a stable for your camels. We used **acacia plank blocks** and **fencing**. Then mark out your starting line. We used a combination of **acacia** and **birch plank blocks** to do that.

STEP 2

To build your race track, go for **fencing**—it works really well! Ours is ten blocks wide.

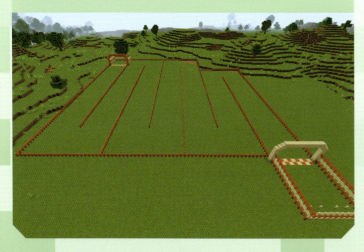

STEP 3

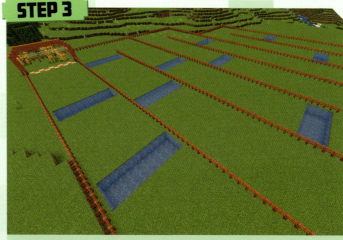

Introduce pools of **water** that are three blocks long. It will mean that your camel can dash over them to the finish for added excitement and challenge!

RACING GAMES

KING OF THE HILL

PLAYER COUNT: 1-10

In this game, players must compete to be King of the Hill by taking on all the challenges of an obstacle course to reach the top of the pyramid first. Do you think YOU have what it takes?

STEP 1

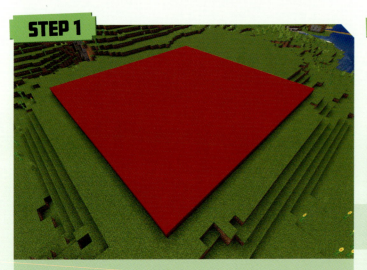

Begin by laying a base for your pyramid. We have used **red concrete blocks** for ours.

STEP 2

Now start to build up your pyramid in layers, leaving a ledge that is two blocks deep for the players to stand or climb on. You can make the sections into different colors, like ours.

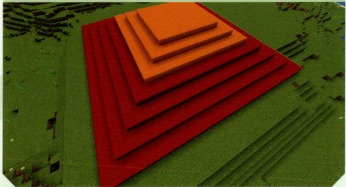

STEP 3

Continue to build up your pyramid. The layers closer to the top have a narrower ledge that is only one block deep. This makes it harder to climb nearer the top!

STEP 4

Place a flag at the top of the pyramid using **fencing** and **wool**. This gives players something to aim toward.

STEP 5

Now the fun can really begin! It's time for you to build dangerous obstacles for your player to navigate. We started by adding random blocks of **lava** . . . look out!

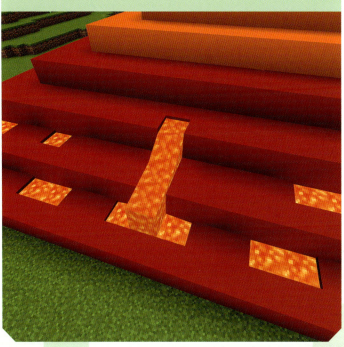

STEP 6

Besides the **lava**, we added **magma blocks**. A player will receive fire damage if they accidentally step on one of these. Ouch!

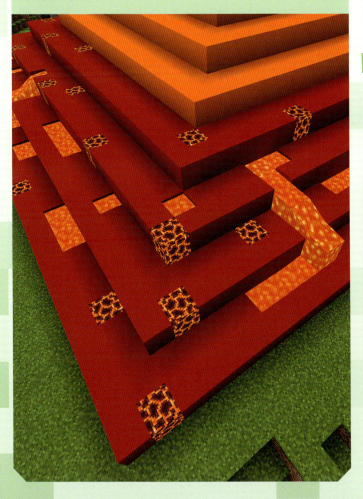

STEP 7

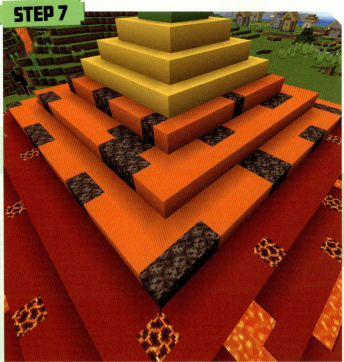

But we didn't stop there. Next we added blocks of **soul sand**. They're a good way to slow players down if they step on them.

RACING GAMES

STEP 8

Another way to effectively slow players down is by adding **cobwebs**. Not only do they add more of a challenge, but they also make it look super spooky and cool. Check it out!

STEP 9

In each corner of the yellow level we added a **pillager**. These guys are fenced in so they won't move from their spot, but they will shoot **arrows** at players as they climb.

STEP 10

Finally, it's a good idea to place **beds** around the edges of your pyramid. Add some small **chests** holding useful items, too!

MINECRAFT MASTER BUILDER: CHALLENGES

RACING GAMES

PLAYER COUNT: 1-10

MICRO PARKOUR MAZE

In this fast-paced game, a simple piece of redstone machinery will time you and your friends as you race through this micro parkour maze. Ready, set . . . RACE!

STEP 1

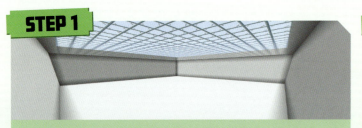

First you will need to build yourself an arena. We used **white concrete blocks** and then covered the top with **glass blocks**.

STEP 2

Lay down a **lever** in a corner of your arena. In front of this, lay down a **sticky piston** with a **block of redstone** attached to it. Then, one block away from this, place a **redstone comparator** and put it in **comparison** mode.

STEP 3

Then add lines of **restone dust** coming out from your **comparator**, like this!

STEP 4

Add another line of **redstone dust** coming away from this and leading to a **redstone repeater**. Add two blocks of **redstone dust** down from this, and then place a block of **concrete** with a **dropper** on top of it.

DID YOU KNOW?

The word parkour derives from parcours du combattant (obstacle course), a classic obstacle course method of military training.

STEP 5

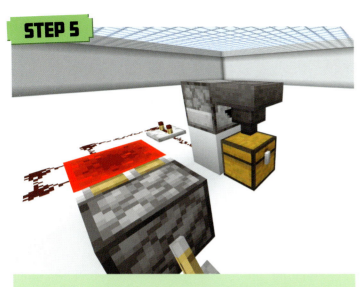

In front of the mouth of your **dropper**, add a **hopper** with a **chest** below it. Fill your **dropper** with any object you choose. Anything that falls from the **dropper** will fall into the **hopper** to be transfered into the **chest**. Once you have run your course, you can check the **chest** to see how long each player has taken to complete the course—just check how many objects they have obtained! (You'll need to play one at a time).

STEP 8

Here are some of our suggestions for inspiration. Here we have included blocks to jump across. Yep, they have **lava** between them!

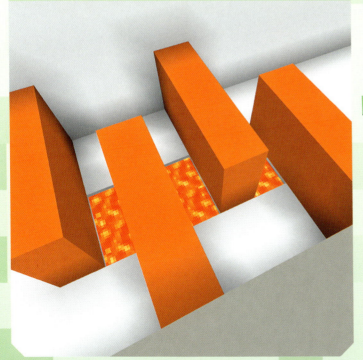

STEP 6

Build walls around your **redstone** circuits. Just make sure you keep the **lever, chest**, and **dropper** open. Now add a start line and a finish line.

STEP 7

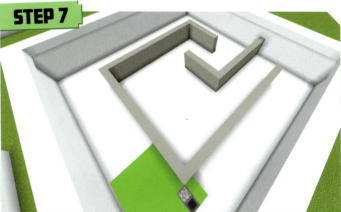

Take some time to plan out a simple course shape. You can lay it out in any way you choose!

STEP 9

And here we have included some **cobwebs** to slow players down. They look awesome, too!

RACING GAMES

STEP 10

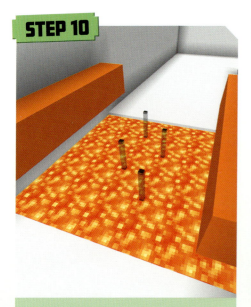

This one is a bubbling **lava** pit. Look closely and you can see tiny **glass panes** arranged for the player to jump across on.

STEP 11

And who doesn't love a maze? We designed a tricky **concrete** maze to navigate.

STEP 12

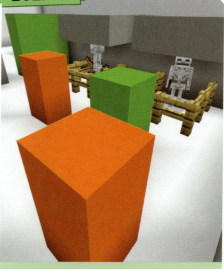

You could also try adding more pillars to creep around while avoiding shooting fenced-in **skeletons**.

STEP 13

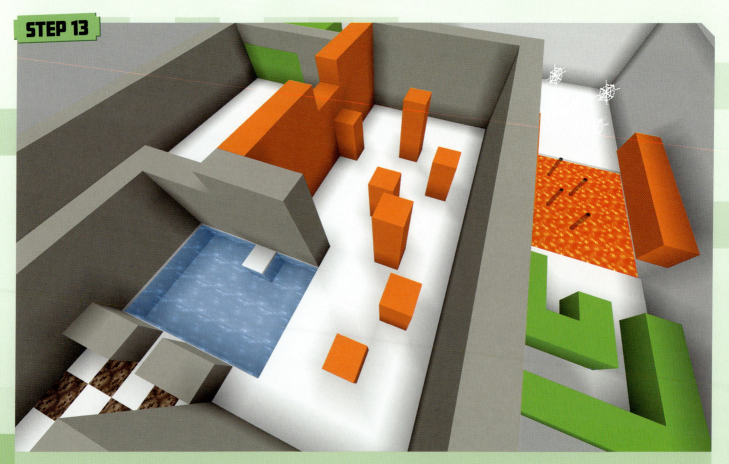

For more ideas, how about **concrete** pillars to jump between, or a pool to swim through? We also threw in blocks of **soul sand** to slow players down.

MINECRAFT MASTER BUILDER: CHALLENGES

STEP 14

Like a challenge? Here is an even more difficult **lava** pool to jump across.

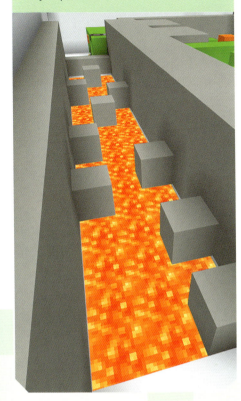

STEP 15

This is a view from above.

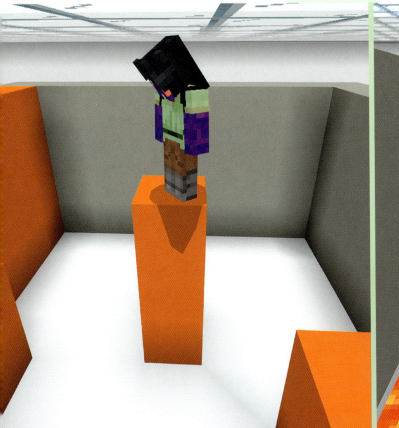

COMBAT GAMES

MINECART JOUSTING

PLAYER COUNT: 2

Here's all you need to build to be ready to play Minecart Jousting! With powered rails, players must try to hit each other as they are pushed back and forth on the tracks. Are YOU ready?

STEP 1

First, use **brick blocks** to create a track for your **minecart**. You will need to create gradual steps upward on each end, like this.

DID YOU KNOW?

Minecarts have a speed limit of eight blocks per second.

STEP 2

Next it's time to lay **rails** over the top of the **brick blocks**. These **rails** should be laid right over the steps at each end to create a slope.

Once you have done this, you can now add a powered rail at each end of the track

STEP 3

Add a **redstone torch** at one end of the track so that the **powered rail** can be constantly charged.

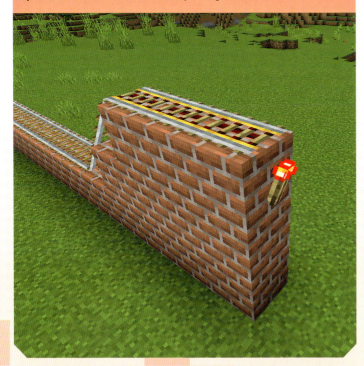

STEP 4

Use **brick blocks** to build a small wall (about four blocks high) around each end of the track. Just make sure it's not overlapping the track you've built!

STEP 5

This is how your **torch** should sit underneath the wall.

STEP 6

The end without the **torch** is your starting end. This is where you need to add a **lever**, as shown below.

Lever

STEP 7

It's a good idea to build up more of a plaftorm around the build at this stage. We have used **stone brick blocks**, but you can use whatever you like!

COMBAT GAMES

STEP 8

Your player will need **armor** and a **chest** with **bows** and **arrows**. You can add these items to the starting end, like this.

Enchant a bow with infinity so that you will not run out of arrows!

STEP 9

Next build some steps at the starting end so that the player is able to enter.

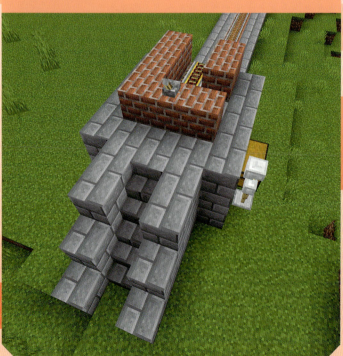

STEP 10

— Minecart

Now you need to add the **minecart**. And don't forget to leave a space for the player to get in.

STEP 11

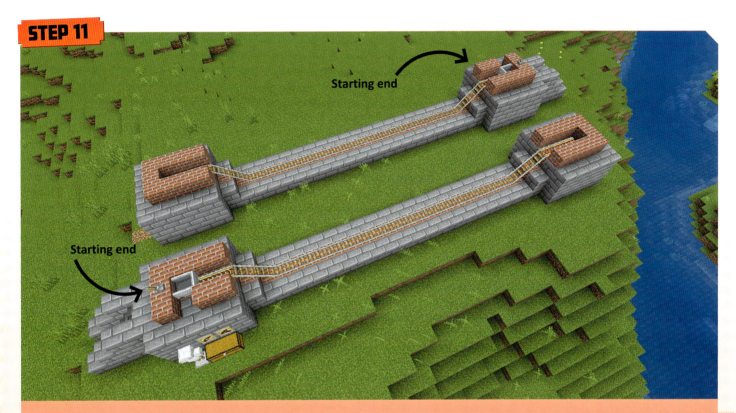

Repeat all of these steps to build the second track, but this time the starting end must be at the opposite end. And it's as simple as that!

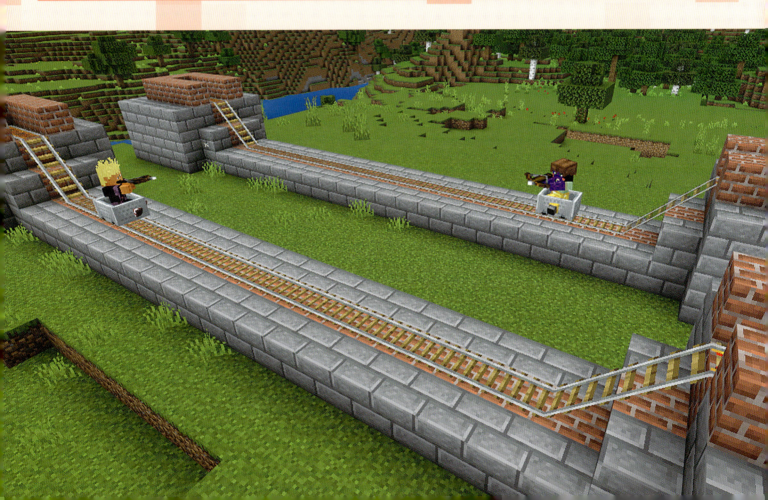

COMBAT GAMES

ICEBOAT COMBAT ARENA

PLAYER COUNT: 2-10

To create an Iceboat Combat Arena, just follow these simple steps. You'll end up with an enclosed arena of packed ice blocks, where players have a weapon and must remain in the boats. Players can win by destroying other boats or players.

STEP 1

First off, you will need to either find or build a large area of **packed ice**.

STEP 2

Once you have done that, lay a large cross in the center. We have used **white concrete blocks** here.

STEP 3

Next, connect up the corners of your cross using the same blocks, like this.

STEP 4

Once you've joined up all of your edges, you will end up with a round shape like this.

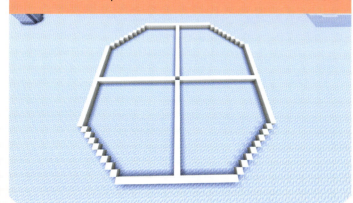

STEP 5

Now you can delete the cross from the center. This will leave you with an impressive arena.

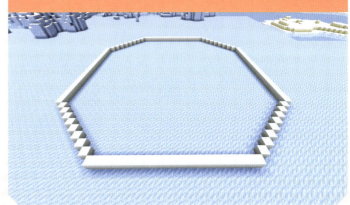

STEP 7

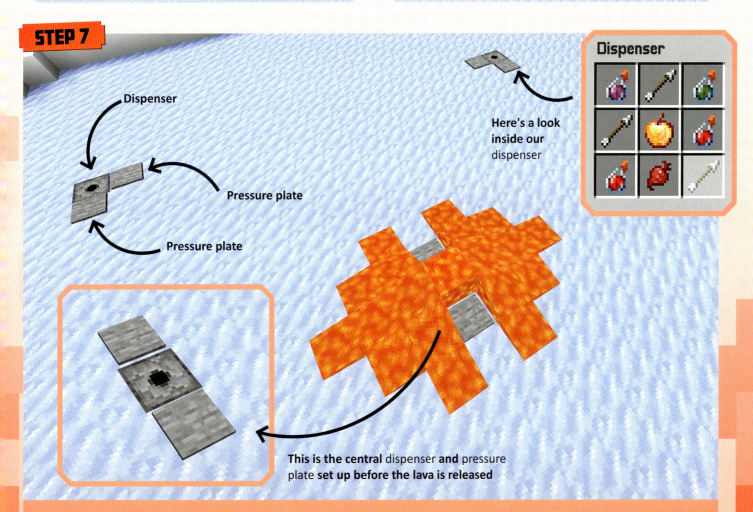

Add a **dispenser** with **pressure plates** on both sides to one corner. When a **boat** passes over it, it will dispense items (both helpful and harmful). We filled our **dispensers** with **arrows**, a **splash potion of healing**, an **enchantment golden apple**, **splash potion of poison**, **splash potion of regeneration** and **beetroot**. Do this in the four corners of your arena. In the center add a **dispenser** with **pressure plates** above and below it. Fill this **dispenser** with **lava** to create a danger point in the middle of your arena.

COMBAT GAMES

STEP 9

Next you need to add a row of **beds** on the outside edge of your arena. This means that when a player is killed they can respawn outside the arena. Then, build up a shelter to go over your **beds**. That looks a bit more cozy!

STEP 9

Add another layer to your arena so that it's a few blocks high. Then add **stairs** to the front section with a **large chest** on each side. Fill one **large chest** with **boats** and the other with helpful items such as **armor**, **weapons**, **food**, **potions**, or **snowballs**. Why not try using the loom to decorate **banners** to hang?

MINECRAFT MASTER BUILDER: CHALLENGES

STEP 10

Here is how your arena should look now you are ready to play!

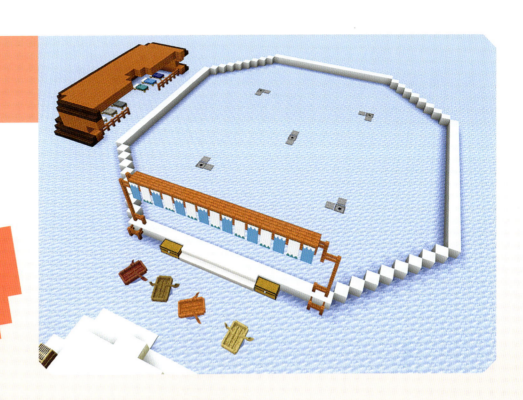

DID YOU KNOW?

Packed ice does not melt if placed near light sources, unlike normal ice.

COMBAT GAMES

SUMOCRAFT

PLAYER COUNT: 2

Players will face each other on platforms and try to knock each other off into the surrounding water! Follow these steps to build everything you need to play.

STEP 1

Dig a circle that is two blocks deep and lay a surface across the bottom. For this, we used **chiseled quartz blocks**. The circle is 17 blocks across at its widest points. It can be any size you want but make sure it is an odd number so there can be a center point.

STEP 2

Then add a frame around the edges, like this. We used **block of quartz**.

STEP 3

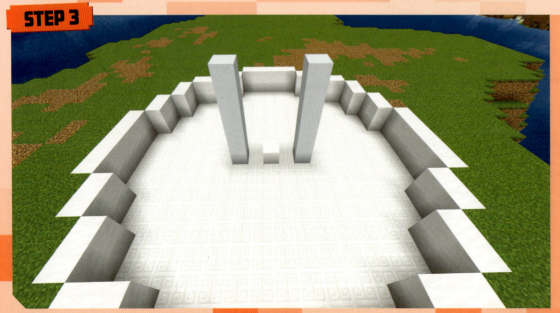

Find the center point and use a temporary marker so you know where it is. You can build your pillars one block out from the center point. They can be as high as you want as long as they are higher than ground level. We used **white concrete blocks**.

MINECRAFT MASTER BUILDER: CHALLENGES

STEP 4

At the top of your pillars, you will need to add two platforms that come outward from the center.

STEP 5

DID YOU KNOW?
In traditional sumo wrestling, a match won't start until both wrestlers have placed both hands on the ground at the same time.

Now it's time to fill the lower level up with **water**.

COMBAT GAMES

STEP 6

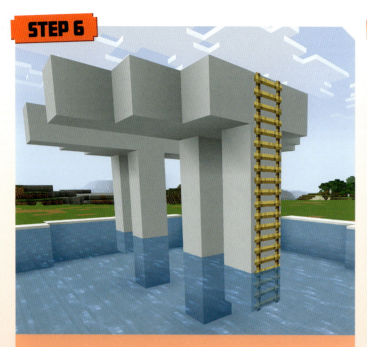

Your players need to be able to climb to the top of the platforms. So add another pillar with a **ladder** at the back of each platform.

STEP 7

Then add your chosen weapon to a **chest** and place this in front of your area. We chose **knockback sticks**—an enchanted stick that can push a player back a few blocks. You can try this or use any non-lethal weapon of your choice.

STEP 8

Add different colored **banners** to each platform to represent each player.

MINECRAFT MASTER BUILDER: CHALLENGES

STEP 9

And last but not least, you can decorate your build however you want!

COMBAT GAMES

FIRE STARTER

PLAYER COUNT: 2-10

Fire Starter is a tribute to the famous Minecraft minigame "Spleef." Here players compete armed with flint and steel! They must set fire to the floor below each other to make the other players drop down into lava.

STEP 1

To begin with, build your bottom platform. This square platform is 38 blocks by 38 blocks. It's two blocks high around the edges, but only one high everywhere else. We used **black concrete blocks** to build ours.

STEP 2

Fill the main part of the platform with **lava**, like this.

STEP 3

From the edge, build a wide track of **ladders** going up into the sky.

STEP 4

At the top of the **ladders**, build a frame that is three blocks wide. We used **yellow concrete blocks**. The gap within the frame needs to be 38 by 38. This means that the frame will be a total of 41 blocks all the way around. These numbers will be important when it comes to coding the **command block** in Step 7.

MINECRAFT MASTER BUILDER: CHALLENGES

STEP 5

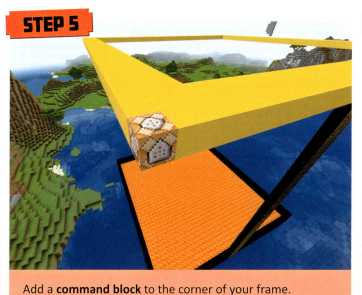

Add a **command block** to the corner of your frame.

STEP 6

Now put a **pressure plate** on top of your **command block**.

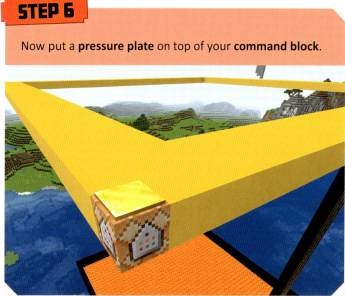

STEP 7

Enter the below code for your **command block**. We are telling the code to move three blocks in from its current position (~3 ~ ~3) and fill the space of 38 blocks by 38 blocks (~41~~41) with **light blue wool**. This coding will help you to set up another game at the end without having to rebuild everything that gets destroyed as the game progresses. If you don't want to use **command blocks**, there is no reason why you can't build everything by hand.

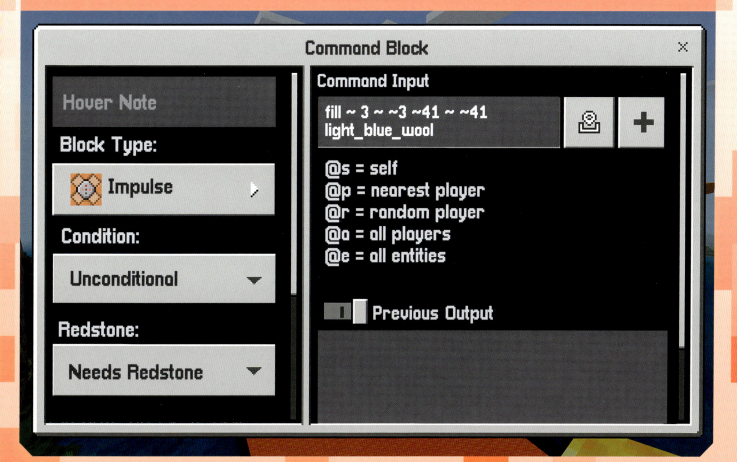

COMBAT GAMES

STEP 8

Simply press down on your **pressure plate** and your frame will be filled with **wool**.

STEP 9

Add some **beds** around the edges of your game so that players can respawn.

STEP 10

This is how the game should look. Awesome!

COMBAT GAMES

PLAYER COUNT: 2-10

SURVIVE THE NIGHT

Get set to build a spooky mansion filled with zombies! The ultimate goal is to survive the night. Think you've got it in you?

STEP 1

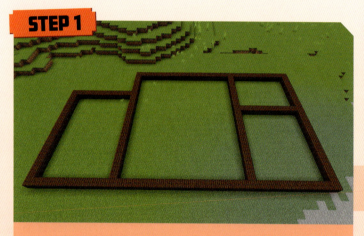

To start with, lay out a base for your spooky mansion and plan out where you would like the rooms to be. We used **dark oak plank blocks**.

STEP 2

Then lay out the flooring—we used **oak plank blocks** for this. Add **stairs** going up to your second floor, and then plan out the windows and doors. We went for door holes without any actual doors.

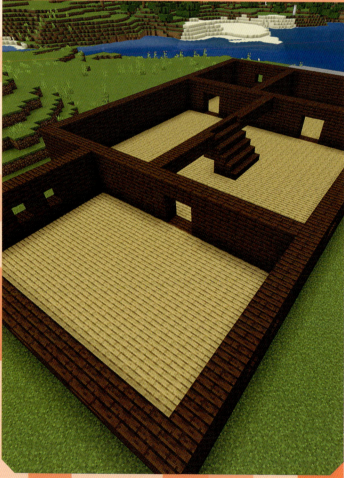

STEP 3

You can build up the second floor of your mansion by using the same technique as you did for the first floor.

While zombies can sometimes break down doors, they will usually keep them out. So, no doors means a much tougher game!

MINECRAFT MASTER BUILDER: CHALLENGES

STEP 4

We opted to build an attic at the top of our mansion. This is a great place to hide our **zombie spawners**!

STEP 5

Next add a roof to your mansion. Each layer should get slightly smaller, like steps, until the sides meet at the top, as shown above.

STEP 6

It's time to decorate the outside of your mansion! We added **cobwebs** and **vines** to make the mansion look extra creepy and abandoned. We also knocked out a few blocks to make holes in the roof to add to the effect.

STEP 7

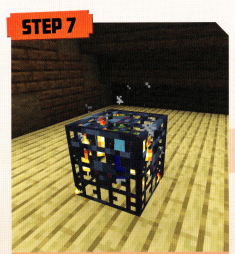

Pop some **zombie spawners** in the attic. We stuck to zombies, but you can add any kind of dangerous mob you like! It is best to avoid creepers, though, because when they explode they will burn your house down.

COMBAT GAMES

STEP 8

You can knock out blocks in the floor or roof and fill them with open **trap doors**. If a zombie sees a hole, it will avoid it, but with a **trap door** they won't see the gaps so will fall through them! You'll have zombies falling down from above when your game starts.

STEP 9

It's a good idea to add some **zombie spawners** outside as well. That way, the zombies will stream in from the front, too!

STEP 10

Decorate your house to up the spooky factor and don't hold back! We added more **cobwebs** inside. Not only do they create a creepy atmosphere, but they also slow down any player (or zombie) that gets caught in them. Handy!

- Spooky painting
- Dragon head
- Cobwebs

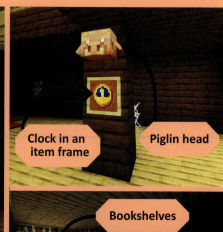

- Clock in an item frame
- Piglin head

- Bookshelves
- Patches of carpet

MINECRAFT MASTER BUILDER: CHALLENGES

STEP 11

Your build is complete. Now you are ready to begin!

STEP 12

To start the game, switch from Creative to Survival mode and set the game to be at night. You can either equip your players with **armor** and **weapons**, or you can give them nothing at all (depending on how much of a challenge you want)!

INVENTORY CHECKLIST

MINI GOLF
- Packed ice
- Brick blocks
- Green carpet
- Snowballs
- A dispenser
- A pressure plate
- Fireworks
- Stone brick blocks
- A hanging sign
- Fencing

CONCRETE POWDER 4
- Glass blocks
- Colored concrete blocks
- Fencing
- Banners
- Large chests
- Colored concrete powder
- Torches
- Pistons
- Redstone dust
- A lever
- A ladder

BATTLE BLAST
- Colored concrete blocks
- Prismarine blocks fencing and stairs
- Hanging signs
- Lecterns
- Chests
- Dispensers
- Colored carpet
- Fireworks
- Levers
- Lanterns

STEVE SAYS
- Stone brick blocks and stairs
- Chiseled stone blocks
- Fencing
- A dispenser
- A pressure plate
- Beds
- Colored concrete blocks
- Fireworks
- Lanterns

GUESS THAT TUNE
- Black concrete blocks
- White concrete blocks
- Emerald blocks (or any other block of your choice—reference the block type sound chart).
- Note blocks
- Pressure plates
- Dark oak plank blocks and stairs

- Signs
- Chests
- A lectern
- A door
- A ladder

BULLSEYE BATTLE
- A target block
- Dispensers
- Redstone dust
- Fireworks
- Bows and arrows

LEAP OF FAITH
- Colored concrete blocks
- Beds
- Fencing
- Slime blocks

ARMOR ARCHERY
- White concrete blocks
- A redstone comparator
- Redstone dust
- Redstone repeaters
- Sticky pistons
- Armor stands
- A lever
- Acacia plank blocks
- Birch stairs
- Birch plank blocks
- Bow and arrows
- Fencing

CHICKEN DROP
- Lava
- Brick blocks
- Oak plank blocks
- Hay bales
- Dispensers
- Redstone dust
- A redstone comparator
- A lever
- Eggs
- Redstone repeaters (optional)
- Glass blocks (optional)
- Banners (optional)
- Fencing (optional)

TNT FLOOR
- Command blocks
- Levers
- Obsidian blocks
- Ladders
- Colored concrete blocks
- Fencing
- TNT block

DANGER BRIDGE
- Colored concrete blocks
- Redstone dust
- Sticky pistons
- Pressure plates

- Polished blackstone brick blocks
- Chiseled stone blocks
- A nether portal

GOLDRUSH
- Sandstone blocks and stairs
- Droppers
- Water
- Apples
- Golden apples
- Redstone dust
- A redstone comparator
- Redstone repeaters
- Purpur blocks

LAVA RACE
- Cobblestone blocks
- Striders
- Warped fungus
- Sticks
- Skeletons
- Blazes
- Piglins
- Magma blocks

CAMEL DASH
- Camels
- Acacia plank blocks and fencing
- Birch plank blocks
- Water

KING OF THE HILL
- Colored concrete blocks
- Fencing
- Wool
- Lava
- Magma blocks
- Soul sand blocks
- Cobwebs
- Pillagers
- Beds
- Chests
- Armor and weapons (optional)

MICRO PARKOUR MAZE
- Colored concrete blocks
- Glass blocks
- Redstone dust
- A redstone comparator
- A sticky piston
- A block of redstone
- A dropper
- A hopper
- A chest
- A lever
- Lava
- Cobwebs
- Glass panes
- Fencing
- Skeletons
- Water
- Soul sand blocks

MINECART JOUSTING
- Brick blocks
- Minecarts
- Redstone torches
- Powered rails
- Rails
- Levers
- Stone brick blocks
- Armor
- Chests
- Bows and arrows

ICE COMBAT ARENA
- Packed ice
- White concrete blocks
- Large chests
- Boats
- Armor
- Weapons
- Food
- Potions
- Snowballs
- Pressure plates
- Dispensers
- Beds
- Banners

SUMOCRAFT
- Chiseled quartz blocks
- Block of quartz blocks
- White concrete blocks
- Water
- Ladders
- Knockback sticks (or any other non-lethal weapons)
- A chest
- Banners

FIRE STARTER
- Colored concrete
- Lava
- Ladders
- A command block
- A pressure plate
- Beds
- Flint and steel

SURVIVE THE NIGHT
- Dark oak plank blocks and stairs
- Oak plank blocks
- Cobwebs
- Vines
- Zombie spawners
- Other hostile mob spawners (optional)
- Trap doors
- Creepy decorations
- Armor (optional)
- Weapons (optional)